Wayne Gretzky

Greatness on Ice

By Jessica Morrison

Crabtree Publishing Company
www.crabtreebooks.com

Crabtree Publishing Company

www.crabtreebooks.com

Author: Jessica Morrison
Publishing plan research and development:
  Sean Charlebois, Reagan Miller
  Crabtree Publishing Company
Editors: Mark Sachner, Lynn Peppas
Proofreader: Wendy Scavuzzo
Indexer: Wendy Scavuzzo
Editorial director: Kathy Middleton
Photo researcher: Ruth Owen
Designer: Alix Wood
Production coordinator: Margaret Amy Salter
Production: Kim Richardson
Prepress technician: Margaret Amy Salter

Written, developed, and produced by
Water Buffalo Books

Publisher's note:
All quotations in this book come from original sources and contain the spelling and grammatical inconsistencies of the original text. The use of such constructions is for the sake of preserving the historical and literary accuracy of the sources.

Photographs and reproductions:
Flickr (Creative Commons): page 1; page 33; page 51; page 55; page 68; page 103 (all)
Getty Images: B. Bennett: page 7; B. Bennett: page 17; Lane Stewart: page 31; Paul Kennedy: page 39; B. Bennett: page 43; B. Bennett: page 59; B. Bennett: page 67; David E. Klutho: page 71; B. Bennett: page 73; B. Bennett: page 81; B. Bennett: page 89; New York Daily News Archive: page 91; Robert Sullivan: page 97
Shutterstock: front cover (background); page 13 (all); page 19; page 20; page 21; page 26; page 29; page 32; page 36; page 42; page 47; page 62; page 77; page 82; page 84; page 95; page 100
Water Buffalo Books: page 9; page 52; page 66; page 70; page 83; page 94
Wikipedia (public domain): front cover (main); page 5; page 15; page 23; page 41; page 57; page 65; page 75; page 85; page 93; page 101

Cover: Wayne Gretzky, the Great One, was always proud to play on Team Canada and represent his home country in international play. Game 2 of the 1987 Canada Cup (now called the World Cup) is considered to be one of the greatest games he ever played in his career.

Library and Archives Canada Cataloguing in Publication

Morrison, J. A. (Jessica A.), 1984-
    Wayne Gretzky : greatness on ice / Jessica Morrison.

(Crabtree groundbreaker biographies)
Includes index.
Issued also in an electronic format.
ISBN 978-0-7787-2539-8 (bound).--ISBN 978-0-7787-2548-0 (pbk.)

    1. Gretzky, Wayne, 1961- --Juvenile literature. 2. Hockey players--Canada--Biography--Juvenile literature.
I. Title. II. Series: Crabtree groundbreaker biographies

GV848.5.G78M67 2011   j796.962092   C2010-903036-2

Library of Congress Cataloging-in-Publication Data

Morrison, Jessica.
  Wayne Gretzky : greatness on ice / Jessica Morrison.
    p. cm. -- (Crabtree groundbreaker biographies)
  Includes index.
  ISBN 978-0-7787-2548-0 (pbk. : alk. paper) --
ISBN 978-0-7787-2539-8 (reinforced library binding : alk. paper) -- ISBN 978-1-4271-9471-8 (electronic (pdf))
  1. Gretzky, Wayne, 1961---Juvenile literature. 2. Hockey players--Canada--Biography--Juvenile literature. I. Title. II. Series.

  GV848.5.M67 2010
  796.962092--dc22
  [B]
                                        2010018112

Crabtree Publishing Company

Printed in the USA/082010/BL20100723

Published in Canada
Crabtree Publishing
616 Welland Ave.
St. Catharines, Ontario
L2M 5V6

Published in the United States
Crabtree Publishing
PMB 59051
350 Fifth Avenue, 59th Floor
New York, New York 10118

Published in the United Kingdom
Crabtree Publishing
Maritime House
Basin Road North, Hove
BN41 1WR

Published in Australia
Crabtree Publishing
386 Mt. Alexander Rd.
Ascot Vale (Melbourne)
VIC 3032

Contents

Chapter 1
A Date with Lord Stanley's Cup

On May 19, 1984, the Edmonton Oilers suited up for game five of the Stanley Cup finals. The locker room was buzzing with anticipation, anxiety, and determination. Despite making it this far, they were not celebrating yet. They had a job to do, and they were all business until their goal was achieved. At the center of the room in jersey number 99 was their star player, Wayne Gretzky. As he finished putting on his equipment, he quickly tucked the right side of his jersey into his pants and made his way to the ice. It was time to play hockey.

Shutting Down the Great One

The Oilers' opponents, the New York Islanders, were defending champions four years running.

Wayne had led the Oilers to victory and their first Stanley Cup win ever.

Over the years, Wayne has always said that winning his first Stanley Cup was his greatest hockey moment.

The Islanders were a tough team and knew exactly what they were up against. They also knew who their most dangerous opponent was. The best hockey player the world had ever seen, the Great One, was their greatest obstacle. For three games, they'd clamped down on Wayne. He didn't score a single goal until game four. The Oilers were still up, three games to one. If they won this game, the title would be theirs.

The young Oilers and veteran Islanders were evenly matched, and both teams remained scoreless in the first period. Then Wayne took over. Grabbing two assists off his teammate Jari Kurri, Wayne sailed the puck past the Islanders' goaltender. By the time the third period clock started counting down the final 20 minutes of the game, the Oilers were ahead. The Islanders played hard and gained another two goals, but it wasn't enough. As the buzzer sounded with a final score of 5–2 for the Oilers, the team stormed the ice. Wayne had led the Oilers to victory and their first Stanley Cup win ever.

Wayne Gretzky, star forward for the Edmonton Oilers, holds the Stanley Cup aloft as he skates a victory lap around the Northlands Arena in Edmonton, Alberta, Canada, on May 19, 1984. When this photo was taken, the Oilers had just defeated the New York Islanders for the National Hockey League championship.

The Greatest Moment

Finally, after years of his watching *Hockey Night in Canada* with his family, and practicing slap shots against his grandparents' barn, the Stanley Cup was his. The sweat-stained jerseys and grueling hours of practice, many of them in the early morning, were worth it. As he hoisted the trophy above his head, 23-year-old Wayne Gretzky achieved what thousands of other players can only dream of—he had a place in the record books.

… everyone was talking about how many games it would take the Great One to reach 50.

Over the years, Wayne has always said that winning his first Stanley Cup was his greatest hockey moment. As team captain, Wayne is now listed first on the Cup's engraving for 1983–1984. Later, he would lead the Oilers to countless more playoff games and three more Stanley Cup wins. Even after his first Stanley Cup win, Gretzky fans watched Wayne go on to even greater record-breaking moments in his career.

STAYING GROUNDED

As one of the most recognized athletes of all time, Wayne Gretzky has had his share of the limelight. It is easy for celebrities and athletes to lose themselves or feel entitled to special status from all their fame. But Wayne is consistently humble and generous to his fans. When asked how he stayed so grounded at the height of his career, Wayne responded:

"I've always felt it was an honor and a privilege to play for your country. You can't make everyone happy ... If you can make your mother and father happy and proud, that's really the only thing you can do. My dad was always in my ear from day one."

This modest attitude has made Wayne one of the most respected athletes in the world.

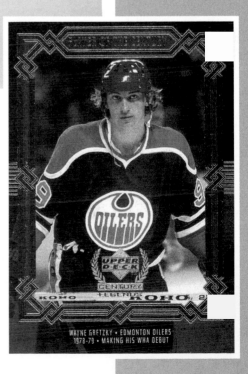

WAYNE GRETZKY • EDMONTON OILERS
1978-79 • MAKING HIS WHA DEBUT

The Toughest Record

Even after four Stanley Cup wins and many record-breaking plays, Wayne believes that the hardest record to beat will be one of his own—scoring 50 goals in 39 games, a record he set back in 1981. As he stepped onto Edmonton's home ice on December 30 of that year, the crowd was abuzz, knowing that he was on his way to making history. He was only 20 years old, but had been playing professional hockey for three years and had been on the ice for an additional 15. With 45 Gretzky goals already racked up in the season, everyone was talking about how many games it would take for the Great One to reach 50. Surely it would take another week or two.

Another goal would secure a win for the Oilers and be a record breaker, all in one.

In the first period, fellow Oiler Paul Coffey banked a shot past the Philadelphia Flyers' net. It went wide, but Wayne saw his chance and flicked the puck past goaltender Pete Peeters. Later in the game, during a four-on-two break, Wayne had control of the puck 20 feet (six meters) away from the Flyers' net.

LINGO OF THE ICE

Like all sports, hockey has its own language. Below are some terms from the world of hockey:

Assist—a pass that immediately precedes a goal.

Blind pass—to pass the puck without looking.

Blue lines—two parallel blue lines that run across the ice, each 60 feet (18 m) from the goal. These lines divide the rink into three zones—the attacking, neutral, and defending zones.

Breakaway—a fast-moving break when a player with the puck clears away from the defensemen and skates in alone toward the goalie.

Deke—a faking motion by the puck handler.

Elbowing—hitting an opponent with an elbow, resulting in a minor penalty.

Face-off—how a play begins. A puck is dropped by the official between the sticks of two opposing players.

Hat trick—three goals scored by one player in a single game.

Icing—a violation that occurs when the puck is shot from behind the red center line across the opponent's goal line.

Offside—a violation that occurs when an attacking player crosses the opponent's blue line before the puck is passed into the attacking zone.

Power play—a play with a team at full strength against a team playing with one man less due to a penalty. The team with fewer men is called "shorthanded."

Roster—a list of players on a team.

Sudden death overtime—an overtime period that ends as soon as the first goal is scored, determining the winner.

Tripping—a minor penalty that occurs when a player places his stick or another part of his body under the feet or legs of an opponent, causing him to fall.

Instead of his usual passing strategy, Wayne fired a slap shot. Peeters could only wish he had seen it coming as he watched it sail past into the net.

Wayne kept his momentum in the second period, skating past the Flyers' defensemen. His anticipation was uncanny. He knew just where he needed to be. By himself at the net, it was one-on-one against Peeters. Peeters was a good goaltender, but he didn't stand a chance against hockey's Great One. Suddenly, Wayne had three goals—a hat trick—and his season total had reached 48 goals.

"When I got to 49, that's when I realized that this was something really special."

Something Special

Goal number 49 came in the third period. The crowd was getting antsy, and Wayne's fellow Oilers were aware of how close he was. The shot came from 20 feet (six meters) away again and blew the fans away. Wayne later remembered, "When I got to 49, that's when I realized that this was something really special."

It was also then that Wayne became determined to beat the record that night. The game was still close. His team was only one goal ahead of the Flyers at 6–5. Another goal would secure a win for the Oilers and be a record breaker, all in one. With ten minutes left in the game, the Flyers were onto him. They stuck close to Wayne, disrupting his plays and blocking every shot. With only a few minutes remaining, the Flyers pulled their goalie from the goal to gain another man on the ice.

With only ten seconds left, Grant Fuhr, the Oilers' goalie, had the puck. He slipped it to Glenn Anderson in front of him, who sent it sailing to Wayne. The Flyers were desperate. With three seconds left on the clock, they tried to charge him before he could get off a shot at the empty net and make history. They were too slow. Wayne slapped the puck forward and watched in anticipation as it struck the back of the net. He had done it—50 goals in 39 games. The previous record holders, Maurice Richard and Mike Bossy, had scored 50 goals in 50 games. Wayne had achieved the same number of goals with 11 games to spare.

The first thing Wayne wanted to do after the game was call his father, Walter. Wayne's dad couldn't have been prouder of his son. At this time the year before, Wayne had scored 17 goals and 56 total points (goals plus assists). Now, he was sitting at 50 goals and 108 points. His coach, Glen Sather, marveled at his young center, saying, "There is no one area that makes him superior. It's a unique combination of all areas."

Chapter 2
Growing into Greatness

Wayne Gretzky was born on January 26, 1961. It was the day hockey legend Gordie Howe scored a goal at the Detroit Olympia in a National Hockey League game, tying up his Detroit Red Wings with the Chicago Black Hawks. Across the border, and just a three-hour drive from Detroit, was the small Canadian town of Brantford, Ontario. On this same cold winter day, another hockey legend, Wayne Gretzky, had just been born.

A True Fan

Walter Gretzky was a real hockey fan. In Canada, hockey is much more than a sport. To many people, it is a way of life. They attend games, crowd around their televisions, and cheer for the teams playing on *Hockey Night in Canada*. A true fan of the game, Walter wanted to make sure his son Wayne enjoyed hockey from the start.

When Wayne was two years old, his father laced up Wayne's first pair of skates. Despite a couple of falls, Wayne took to skating almost immediately. After all, he had been practicing in socked feet on the living room floor since he could stand. To help him learn stick handling,

Walter gave his son a full-sized hockey stick that was cut down to size.

Wayne spent nearly every minute devoted to skating and hockey. For hours, he would circle around empty bleach containers, laughing, smiling, shooting, deking, and falling down. At the end of the day, Wayne came inside for a warm dinner and talked more about hockey with his father. Whenever he wasn't inside watching the latest games with his family, he was outside skating at nearby rinks.

Cold Ice, Warm Kitchen

The biggest problem Walter encountered during his son's learning years was simple: It was cold! While Wayne practiced on neighborhood ice rinks, Walter often waited and watched in the car. To avoid the bitter cold during Wayne's practice, Walter decided to build a rink in the family's backyard. When Wayne was four, Walter ran the lawn sprinkler on the frozen ground all night long. In the morning, a perfect patch of ice was waiting for Wayne. Finally, Walter and his wife could watch their son play hockey from the warmth

A true fan of the game, Walter wanted to make sure his son Wayne enjoyed hockey from the start.

A young Wayne Gretzky poses in his Hespeler minor novice team uniform, around 1974 in Ontario, Canada.

of the kitchen. The Gretzky family called the backyard rink "The Wally Coliseum" in honor of Walter. He remembers, "It was for self-preservation, I got sick of taking him to the park and sitting there for hours freezing to death."

For four winters, Wayne continued to practice the game in Wally Coliseum. He learned to weave tightly around empty detergent bottles and fired slap shots against

When Wayne was four, Walter ran the lawn sprinkler on the frozen ground all night long. In the morning, a perfect patch of ice was waiting for Wayne.

the side of his grandparents' farmhouse. He broke countless hockey sticks in the process, but his parents always supplied him with a fresh stick each month. In the early years, Wayne's life was all about hockey.

Small—and Great—for His Age

Then Wayne hit a wall. He had spent years practicing his skills and playing pickup games with neighbors, but now he wanted to play a real game. At this point, five-year-old Wayne could skate circles around many players twice his age. But rules were rules, and none of the youth leagues in the area would accept a player younger than ten. Finally, at the age of six, Wayne was allowed to try out for the Brantford Atom League to play for the Nadrofsky Steelers. The weight differences were huge at that age, and Wayne was a far cry from the 185 pounds (84 kilograms) he would reach at the peak of his career. But Wayne powered through the tryout, and the coaches were immediately impressed. In 1967, Wayne put on his first jersey—number 11.

Even for a six-year-old, Wayne was very small for his age. Compared to his teammates, he looked even smaller. His hockey jersey

nearly reached the ice, and Wayne often got his stick caught because it was so long. To help him with this, Walter tucked the jersey into his pants on the shooting side. At the time, it was a simple wardrobe solution. But it was also a style that Wayne would sport for the rest of his career.

Wayne certainly wasn't the biggest player on the team (in fact, he was the smallest), and he wasn't the fastest. Wayne's coaches allowed him on the team because of his stick handling. Once he had the puck, it was virtually impossible for the other players to take it from him. But he still struggled as a smaller kid playing with older boys. While playing for the Atoms, Wayne scored only one goal during his first year. His father Walter was criticized at the end of the season for encouraging such an undersized child to play with the larger, better kids. At the end of the season, Wayne didn't receive any awards. Wayne remembers, "Everybody won a trophy but me." His parents told him to keep working, and someday he would have more trophies than he had room for. Wayne listened to his parents and kept practicing hard, despite his disappointment at not having received a trophy.

In the following season, Wayne was still small for the game, but his scoring totals were rising fast. He skated quickly around the older boys and scored 27 goals. He also received his first-ever honor, the Wally Bauer Trophy for the most improved Novice All-Star. Audiences wondered how such a small boy could be scoring against larger ten-year-olds.

In his third year, Wayne scored 104 goals,

and many parents around the league insisted that the season had been a fluke. They were

In just 85 games, Wayne gained national attention by scoring 378 goals. It was official—Wayne was a prodigy.

uncomfortable about his performance and believed there was no way Wayne would do that again. They were right. In his fourth year, instead of reaching 104 goals at the end of the season, Wayne achieved this in half a season, finishing with 196 goals overall.

A Ten-Year-Old Prodigy

Wayne's scoring totals were starting to blow the league away. His father asked him if he would like to continue playing novice for another year or move up to Peewee level. Wayne chose to stay in novice, and he was ten years old during his final season. In just 85 games, Wayne gained national attention by scoring 378 goals. It was official—Wayne was a prodigy. Reporters wanted to interview him, stories about him appeared in the sports media, and fans asked him for autographs.

It wasn't just Wayne's accurate shots and clean skating that impressed audiences. Wayne had incredible anticipation. He always seemed

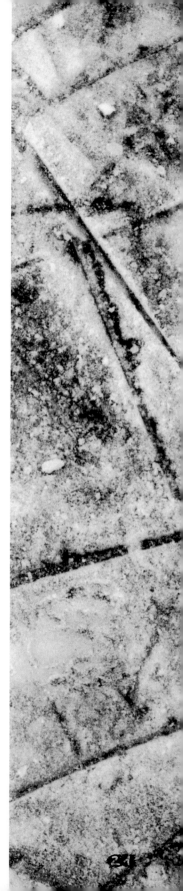

to know where the puck was going a few seconds before it got there. A sportswriter in London, Ontario called him "The Great Gretzky," a name that stuck with Wayne for life, along with "The Great One," which is how Wayne came to be known as a pro. He was also nicknamed the "White Tornado" because of the white gloves he wore. Many thought this was to be showy, but they were very light and fit comfortably on his smaller frame.

Paying the Price

Fame has its price, and soon Wayne was over-whelmed with all the media attention. Off the ice, Wayne would even switch jackets with his friend and goalie Greg Stefan, to avoid it. For every parent who loved watching his talent there was another who was jealous of his ability. Some of his teammates were resentful of his skills and accused him of showboating. Although he had a high assist total, they accused him of hogging the puck. During introductions, Wayne was even booed. His coach and uncle, Bob Hockins, was also criticized for playing Wayne so much. Often, Wayne's playing time was 40 minutes out of a 45-minute game. Although he loved hockey, all of the attention made Wayne soon realize that it was becoming more than a game.

Hockey was not the only sport Wayne played, and it was not the only one in which he had to take abuse because of his talents. He also played baseball, basketball, and lacrosse, but he was not a star in these sports. In fact, he recalls that he loved baseball "probably even more than hockey." Although he was a good

MEETING AN IDOL: GORDIE HOWE

9

Born in 1928, Gordie Howe was one of the all-time greats of hockey. Wishing to be just like his idol, Wayne initially wanted jersey number 9. When he was ten years old, he was interviewed in a local paper, where he talked about his idol:

"Gordie Howe is my kind of player. He had so many tricks around the net, no wonder he scored so many goals. I'd like to be just like him."

A year after that interview, Wayne got to attend a "Great Men of Sports" dinner held in his town, with Howe sitting at the head table. He told Wayne to keep working on his backhand. Howe also came to the rescue when Wayne was unexpectedly asked to say a few words to the group. Going up and putting his arms around the young player, Howe said that anyone who had already done what Wayne had done didn't need to say a word. Wayne heaved a big sigh of relief and grinned, feeling confirmed in his adoration of Mr. Hockey. To Wayne, Howe represented not only amazing hockey skills but also sportsmanship, integrity, and manners. It was a moment he would never forget.

team player, parents and opposing coaches would often hassle him when he played these other sports. It didn't last long, however. Although Wayne liked baseball and his other sports, he just couldn't throw hockey away, and he soon gave up playing other sports.

Despite the distractions of jealous players and parents, Wayne continued to play his game well. In 1972, he moved to the Peewee

Wayne played incredibly well and earned himself another nickname— "Le Grand Gretzky."

League, playing for Turkstra Lumber for two years. During his first year, he scored 105 goals and, in his second year, he scored 192 goals. His last year of hockey in Brantford was playing for the Charon Chargers. In 1974, 13-year-old Wayne and his team played the Quebec International Pee-Wee Hockey Tournament. This was a large tournament, featuring the best teams in North America. It was also Wayne's first taste of international hockey. In his first game at the Colisée, Wayne added four assists and scored seven goals. Although his team was knocked out during the semi-finals, Wayne played incredibly well and earned himself another nickname—"Le Grand

Gretzky." After the game, fans waited outside the team's dressing room for autographs.

A Great Escape

Wayne wanted to play hockey, but the small town of Brantford followed his every move. It soon became clear that all of the negative attention was hurting him. Often, the criticism brought Wayne to the point of tears. Angry, jealous parents and fans were getting to be too much to handle.

In 1975, Wayne was given a chance at a more normal life.

Ontario has helped train more NHL players than any other country, province, or state in the world. It is also home to the Metro Toronto Hockey League (now the Greater Toronto Hockey League), the largest minor-level amateur hockey association in the world. Wayne's parents wanted him to play in Toronto, but it meant making some big changes. Toronto was about 60 miles (97 kilometers) from his hometown, but Wayne was eager to escape. Wayne's parents arranged for a teammate's parents—Bill and Rita Cornish—to become his legal guardians during his stay. Living with them, he could play hockey and attend school in Toronto.

Aiming High

Although many believed he left for the city only to play hockey, Wayne would later remember that he "just wanted to escape the pressures." After enrolling in school and transferring leagues, Wayne looked forward to his new start. He was hoping to join the Toronto Young Nationals, but the Ontario Minor Hockey Association (OMHA) wouldn't allow it. They said he would play for his hometown league in Brantford or none at all.

Wayne fought this decision and refused to return home, but he finally conceded to joining Toronto's Metro Junior B Team, the Vaughan

Wayne was so eager to be "normal" that he didn't tell his classmates he was a hockey player.

Nationals. The Nats were not under the control of the OMHA, so Wayne was free to join without any legal problems. The Nats were in a league for older players, and Wayne would now be playing against boys four age groups above his own. At 14, Wayne would now be playing against 20-year-olds.

Up to the Challenge

Wayne was used to the challenge. For the first time since he began playing in organized hockey games, Wayne was free from hassles and worry. Nobody booed him or yelled nasty comments from the stands. At school, he was a regular student and nobody asked for his autograph. Wayne was so eager to be "normal" that he didn't tell his classmates he was a hockey player.

On the ice, a newly energized Wayne also excelled. During his first season, he scored 27 goals and earned 33 assists. Soon, he added another trophy to his collection by earning the league's Rookie of the Year award. After his first season with the Nats, he was called up to play with the Peterborough Petes three times. In 1976, the *Peterborough Examiner* featured a full story on his arrival and reviewed the game two days later:

"Gretzky, up from the ... Nationals of the Metro Junior B League in Toronto, fired a good pass to Tim Trimper, who scored the winning goal.... The high-scoring 15-year-old took a regular shift with Trimper and Bill Leaman and the line played extremely well, not looking the least bit out of place."

During his three games with the Petes, Wayne impressed not only fans but also the coach, Garry Young.

After two years away from his family, Wayne missed home and was often lonely, but there was no denying that his skills on the ice were improving. Soon, scouts were watching Wayne, and at the age of 16, he was finally eligible for the Ontario Hockey Association draft. His family was getting very anxious to find out which team would draft him and how far from home he would be. To help keep his son closer, Walter wrote letters to several of the distant teams, asking them not to select his son.

The Peterborough Petes wanted to draft Wayne using their fourth draft pick and made deals with both Oshawa and Kitchener so they would not select him. They didn't make a deal

Soon scouts were watching Wayne and, at the age of 16, he was finally eligible for the Ontario Hockey Association draft.

with the Sault Ste. Marie Greyhounds, however, thinking they were far enough away that they wouldn't be as familiar with Wayne's reputation. The Petes were wrong, and he was the Greyhounds' first draft pick.

A Trip to the Soo

Located in Sault Ste. Marie, a northern Ontario town of about 32,000, the Greyhounds were a Major Junior A team, which made them a very high minor-level amateur team. When Wayne was drafted, he and his father drove to Sault Ste. Marie to speak to Angelo Bumbacco, the general manager, to tell him that Wayne wouldn't play there. With the head coach, Muzz MacPherson, assuring Wayne that he would receive plenty of ice time, Bumbacco managed to convince Wayne and his dad to reconsider their position on not playing for the Greyhounds. To seal the deal, Bumbacco also promised that the team would pay for Wayne's college education if Wayne was ever hurt or cut from the Greyhounds. Wayne and his family were convinced and he officially joined the team in 1977, with a salary of $25 a week plus expenses.

Wayne tried to get jersey number nine in honor of his hero, Gordie Howe, but Coach MacPherson wouldn't take it from an older player to give to rookie Wayne. Instead, he offered Wayne the number 19, which didn't appeal to him. MacPherson knew just what to do. He remembered that the great Phil Esposito had to give up his lucky number seven when he joined the Boston Bruins. His solution was to double his favorite number and turn it into 77. When MacPherson offered Wayne the same chance—to double the number nine—he had a hand in creating hockey history with the creation of the now-legendary 99.

Junior A

Junior A hockey is often the last shot that many hockey players have at joining the National Hockey League. The hours are grueling and the playing can be dirty. In Junior A, every young man has big dreams of being drafted into the NHL. They are playing hard, hoping to attract attention and gain respect. During his Junior A time, Wayne's life was a blur. He went to school during the day, but the rest of his time was devoted to practice and games. Many games were away, which meant road trips and

long hours into the night. Nonetheless, Wayne excelled during his first game with the Greyhounds, scoring three goals and adding three assists against the Oshawa Generals. Throughout the season, he even broke the league's old scoring record with 182 points. Despite these numbers, Wayne wasn't the lead scorer that year. Bobby Smith also broke the record, with 192 points.

Wayne was also invited to play for Team Canada at the World Junior Championships, visiting Quebec again. As with his first visit to Quebec, he was embraced by the crowd as he

Wayne's simple, yet effective, vision of playing hockey led him to finish the season with 70 goals.

played in one of the most talented teams ever to grace the World Juniors. The team finished third overall, but Wayne scored eight goals and added 17 points in only six games. Part of his success lay in the simplicity with which he saw the game:

"People talk about skating, puck handling, and shooting, but the whole sport is angles ... Basically, my whole game is angles."

Wearing his now-legendary number 99, Wayne Gretzky moves the puck down the ice for the Sault Ste. Marie Greyhounds against the Hamilton Fincups. This game was played in January 1978. Six months later, he would be a member of the Indianapolis Racers of the World Hockey Association.

THE NUMBER 99

Wayne's first hockey number was 11. Later, when he joined the Greyhounds, Wayne wanted to become number nine, in honor of his hockey hero, Gordie Howe. Unfortunately, number nine was taken by another player. When Wayne and his coach decided on 99, some fans considered his choice to be a slap in the face to the game's traditional use of lower numbers. Once again, Wayne found himself being criticized, this time for supposedly being arrogant.

As if to silence his critics, on the first night that he wore 99, Wayne scored three goals. The number 99 soon became synonymous with Wayne Gretzky. Now a part of hockey tradition in its own right, number 99 has even spread into other games. In poker, a pair of nines is often known as a "Gretzky."

Wayne Gretzky's 99 jersey, worn during the inaguaral World Cup in 1996. It is on display in the Hockey Hall of Fame in Toronto, Ontario.

GRETZKY

99

Wayne's simple, yet effective, vision of playing hockey led him to finish the season with 70 goals, coming in second to Bobby Smith of the Ottawa 67's. Smith was a year older

At 17, the Great Gretzky was ready to go pro, but it wasn't the NHL that would inherit Wayne from Junior A.

than Wayne and was first to be drafted in the NHL's 1978 Entry Draft.

Wayne was also looking forward to moving up a league. When Coach MacPherson decided to leave the Greyhounds, Wayne was even more motivated to seek out a new level. At 17, the Great Gretzky was ready to go pro, but it wasn't the NHL that would inherit Wayne from Junior A.

Moving Up to the WHA

The world of hockey changed in 1972, with the establishment of the World Hockey Association. This was the only serious rival the National Hockey League had seen since the old Western Hockey League collapsed in 1926. Although it only lasted seven years, the WHA made a clear impression on players. By signing young talent early on, the WHA nabbed many of the stars who would otherwise have gone to the NHL.

THE WORLD HOCKEY ASSOCIATION

The World Hockey Association (WHA) was a professional ice hockey league founded in 1971 by Gary Davidson and Dennis Murphy. Competing directly against the National Hockey League, the WHA wanted to attract players with its willingness to pay higher salaries than the NHL. During its first year, 67 players jumped to the WHA from the NHL, including Bobby Hull. Hull was one of the greatest skaters in the game, who left the Chicago Black Hawks to play for the upstart Winnipeg Jets. Twelve teams were formed, including teams from cities without NHL teams.

Despite its good intentions, the WHA was shaky from the start. Many teams folded or relocated, often in the middle of the season. Financial troubles plagued the league for years and, by 1976, it became obvious the WHA could not sustain itself. Three years later, in 1979, after numerous merger plans were announced and derailed, a merger with the NHL was finally approved. Actually, the deal was less a merger and more of an absorption into the NHL of four WHA teams, the Quebec Nordiques, Winnipeg Jets, New England Whalers, and Edmonton Oilers. The teams were regarded more as "expansion" teams than as established franchises on a par with the older NHL teams. Despite this downgrading of the WHA teams' stature within the NHL, and despite the fact that the league disintegrated, numerous hockey greats made their debut in the WHA, including Mark Messier and Mike Gartner. Of course, when the Oilers joined the NHL, they brought Wayne Gretzky with them.

Many future hockey superstars got their start in the WHA, including Mike Howe (Gordie Howe's son), Ken Linseman, Mike Gartner, and Mark Messier. After a year with the Soo Greyhounds, the 17-year-old Gretzky received his first shot at the big time from the WHA.

During his year with the Soo, Wayne had developed an intense fear of flying from the small planes that transported the team from town to town. In June of 1978, a very nervous Wayne signed a "personal services" contract on a flight with Indianapolis Racers owner Nelson Skalbania. Luckily, his new salary would give him an incentive to fly. Wayne was set to earn $825,000 with the Racers, a far cry from the $5 an hour summer job patching potholes he held a year earlier.

Despite his anticipated talent within the new league, Wayne experienced quite a culture shock in Indianapolis. Indianapolis was a city with no hockey tradition at all, unlike hockey-crazed Canada. Instead of hockey, wintertime in Indianapolis meant basketball. The Racers tried to drum up hockey interest by sending Wayne out on personal appearances, signing autographs, and selling tickets. Indianapolis wasn't Brantford, however, and Wayne's presence drew little interest.

Game attendance wasn't much better. The Racers drew only 11,000 fans for their season opener, and attendance dropped even further from then on to an average of 6,000 per game. After eight games, Skalbania was losing a lot of money on the Racers. He decided to auction Gretzky to the Winnipeg Jets or the Edmonton Oilers. Whichever team could pay $200,000 first would land a contract with Wayne. Edmonton answered Skalbania's call and, on his 18th birthday, Wayne signed a contract and headed for Edmonton to join the Oilers. Few could have anticipated the effect this move would have on Wayne, the Oilers, or the world of professional hockey.

Gretzky and the Oilers

It was January 1979 and, at the time, the Oilers were still members of the WHA. Edmonton was a hockey-crazy town, and local fans were ready for the skilled center to join their team. With ticket sales soaring, nobody knew what to expect from Wayne. There were even rumors that the Oilers would soon be asked to join the NHL.

"One day, we're going to be in the NHL, and you're going to be captain of this team."

Edmonton coach Glen Sather was also ready for Wayne. When he first saw Wayne, he thought he was one of the players' kids. He was still only 17, the youngest player by three years. But Sather had high hopes and didn't hold back his opinion from young Wayne: "One day, we're going to be in the NHL, and you're going to be captain of this team." He even allowed Wayne to stay with him and his family until he found a permanent home. Wayne was stunned by this positive attention. Oilers owner Peter Pocklington was also eager for Wayne to join his team. He signed him before even seeing him play and ordered a giant cake to be served on center ice alongside Wayne's contract.

Joining the Oilers for the last 72 games of the season, Wayne led the team to a first-place finish in the six-team league. Edmonton lost the championship to the Winnipeg Jets, four games to two. With 110 points and 46 goals, Wayne finished third in the WHA and earned Rookie of the Year. Although fans didn't know it at the time, this would be the last WHA championship before the league dissolved. After the 1978–1979 season, four of the six WHA teams joined the NHL, including the Edmonton Oilers. It was official. Number 99 and the world's most respected hockey league were about to become acquainted.

Opposite: Edmonton Oiler Wayne Gretzky with head coach Glen Sather during a practice in September 1981

Chapter 3
A Career in Full Flight

Nobody knew what to expect from Wayne and the Oilers during their first official games in the NHL in 1979. Wayne was a lot smaller than most of the other NHL players, which could be a major drawback during rough play. Many wondered if the 18-year-old could handle the pressure of playing against the world's best players. They needn't have worried. Wayne's upbringing and integrity gave him a level head during stress. "I've had pressure all along," he remembers. "There's always going to be pressure … I can't think about it."

New to the NHL

Experts believed the four WHA teams would have a rough start, and they weren't entirely wrong. Wayne didn't score a goal until the team's fifth game, and he had to learn to deal with a grueling schedule. He remembers thinking after that first goal, "If I never play in the NHL again, at least I scored a goal." There would be 80 games across North America, which took the team on countless long road trips. Making matters worse, Wayne suffered from tonsillitis and was often unable to speak.

Soon after his rough start, things started to pick up. Along with Wayne, the Oilers also acquired center Mark Messier and defenseman Kevin Lowe. The three became best friends and formed the core of the Oilers. Wayne had also made a habit of proving doubters wrong, and he was determined to do the same in the NHL. By the All-Star break, he was showing fans what the fuss was all about. He piled up the points, scoring seven points in a single game against Montreal. This was one point shy of the NHL single-game record. By April 1980, Wayne had scored his 50th goal. At 19 years old, he was the youngest player in the history of the NHL to do so. Reaching 137 points by the end of the season, Wayne tied Marcel Dionne of the Los Angeles Kings for most total points (goals plus assists) of the season. Dionne's total included two more actual goals scored, and so the league awarded him the Art Ross Trophy for most total points. Wayne got a pleasant surprise at the season's end, however, when he was awarded the Hart Memorial Trophy as the league's Most Valuable Player. He was also given the league's sportsmanship award for his behavior on and off the ice.

Wayne had also made a habit of proving doubters wrong, and he was determined to do the same in the NHL.

Wearing his famous number 99 for the Edmonton Oilers, Wayne Gretzky slips the puck past Don Edwards, goalie for the Buffalo Sabres, during an NHL game in Buffalo on February 24, 1982. With this goal, Wayne broke the NHL scoring record.

In keeping with his sportsmanlike attitude, Wayne was careful about his attitude toward his awards. When Dionne was given the league's scoring title, Wayne was gracious about not being allowed to share the award, but he also noted that giving goals more importance than assists might send the wrong message to youngsters: "I still think an assist is as important as a goal." In other words, Wayne believed that helping others achieve their goals was just as important as achieving your own. It was his attitude that earned him the Lady Byng Trophy in 1979 for gentlemanly play and the respect of most other players on the ice.

Wayne believed that helping others achieve their goals was just as important as achieving your own.

The Oilers had a season for the record books, as did their star center. They made it to the playoffs, where they were swept by the Philadelphia Flyers. Although losing three games to none looked bad on paper, the Oilers played incredibly well, forcing the Flyers into one overtime period in game one and two overtimes before succumbing in game three. After his first season, few people doubted that

Gretzky was made for the NHL. Coach Sather realized that by building the team around Wayne, the Oilers would reach new heights.

The 1980–1981 season opened with the Oilers feeling hungry for more. Coach Sather had picked up Paul Coffey, Andy Moog, and Jari Kurri in the off-season. These new players gave Wayne the chance to execute his playmaking abilities.

It was also during this season that fans and coaches began to notice Gretzky's incredible skill behind the net. His stick handling in "Gretzky's office," as they called it, confused opponents and drove fans wild. Wayne learned this skill while still in Junior B, when he was too small to stay in front of the goal. His coach at the time told him to stake out behind the net, a move that was rarely seen in the NHL. By staying behind the net, he could easily backhand a goal in or, more likely, pass to a teammate in front who was open. Fresh with new players and blossoming skill, the Oilers made the playoffs again.

AGENT 99 MAKES HEADLINES

During his first year with the Oilers, Wayne wasn't always called the Great One. To commentators and the media, he was known by other nicknames, such as Agent 99, The Franchise, and The Kid. As the season rolled on, Wayne proved he was destined for more than 15 minutes of fame. Oilers owner Peter Pocklington would later reveal he had been offered two million dollars for Wayne. At that time, Pocklington swore he'd turn down any offer for Wayne, saying, "There is no price on greatness."

The Miracle in Montreal

First up against the Oilers were the Montreal

Canadiens. Even Coach Sather didn't actually think the Oilers, who had finished in third place in their division, could beat first-place Montreal, and he tried to prepare his team mentally for the game by telling them they had nothing to lose.

Although losing in the second round was a big disappointment, the Oilers and the Great One had won fans for life.

Wayne wasn't quite ready to fall prey to the disaster that everyone else called imminent. After reading in the papers that Montreal's goalie had promised that the Canadiens' Guy LaFleur would put Gretzky "in his back pocket," Wayne was determined. In their first game against the Canadiens, Wayne came up with five assists and led the team to a 6–3 win. After the last goal, Wayne calmly skated past the Montreal bench and lightly tapped the back pocket of his pants as a sign that he was fully aware of—and enjoying—the moment!

After losing to the Oilers, the Canadiens were in a state of shock. When they lost again in the second game, they were even more shocked. Wayne knew that the Oilers were close to pulling off something really big, and he refused to let the opportunity to sweep

Montreal slip away. In game three, Wayne scored a hat trick and added an assist, leading the Oilers to victory with a 6–2 win. The "Miracle in Montreal" was one of the biggest upsets in NHL history.

The next round took the Oilers to Long Island to face the New York Islanders. The Oilers felt as if they were on a roll but, in the Islanders, they met an experienced team with players in their prime. The Islanders knew how to play well under pressure and weren't going to let Wayne take over. They finally dominated the Oilers, beating them four games to two. Edmonton had nothing to be ashamed of. This former WHA team took the eventual winner of the Stanley Cup to six games. Although losing in the second round was a big disappointment, the Oilers and the Great One had won fans for life. Wayne also demonstrated that he was only getting better as he won his second MVP award. He later wrote, "I was proving I could stay with anybody. The Soo seemed a million miles away."

The Road to the Cup

On top of Wayne's skill on ice, he believed it was always important to represent himself and his country well. Whenever he had a chance, he promoted the game of hockey to the rest of the world, gaining fans and respect in the process. In the off-season during 1981, Wayne was asked to represent his country in the Canada Cup. This is an international tournament that occurs every four years. Gretzky and the team were a favorite to win, and the players had a lot of pressure on their shoulders.

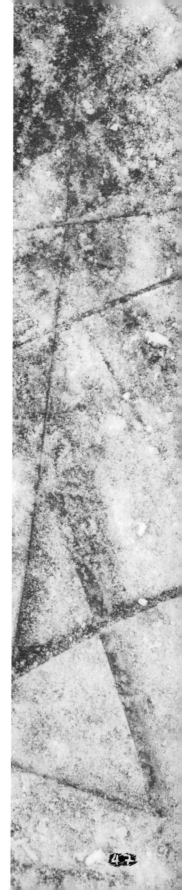

During the tournament, Wayne racked up
the points, helping his team beat Finland and
the United States with 9–0 and 8–3 totals. In
the championship game, however, they were
defeated 8–1 by the Soviet Union. Wayne led
all the players in scoring, but he felt this was
one of the most embarrassing losses of his
career. He admitted his failure and said he
had "played so badly they should have sent
me to Siberia."

He wasn't to be disappointed for long. The
new 1981–1982 season began, and the records
began to fall. Wayne had the most dominant
season by one player in the history of the game.
He scored 92 goals and 120 assists, resulting in

*The Islanders dove for the puck and basically
"sacrificed" themselves for each win ... Wayne
recalls seeing the Islanders' blackened eyes and
bloody mouths in the locker room ...*

212 points—a point total that had previously
been unfathomable. He even scored 50 goals
in 39 games, a record that Wayne feels will be
the hardest to break. Nobody in the NHL had
ever scored 50 goals in fewer than 50 games,
and he had done it with 11 to spare. With these
numbers, Wayne didn't just break records.

THE EINSTEIN OF HOCKEY

At six feet (183 centimeters) tall and 185 pounds (84 kg), Wayne was not a large or physically commanding hockey player. He wasn't extraordinarily quick, nor did he have the strongest shot. Critics, coaches, and fans soon learned that Wayne's strength did not lie in any ordinary hockey skill. Instead, Wayne had a "rink sense" that allowed him to play at a level that was far above other players'. He could not only envision the whole rink in his mind and how players were moving within it, he could anticipate where the puck was going two or three seconds before it happened. This uncanny ability allowed Wayne to sense when another teammate was about to get possession of the puck so he could position himself for a pass. Along with anticipating where the puck was going, Wayne could also see body checks coming and avoid them before he was hit into the boards. Because of his "vision," Wayne was sometimes called the "Einstein of Hockey."

He blew them out of the water! He had changed what people thought was possible in hockey. Coach Sather marveled at his young center, saying, "There is no one area that makes him superior. Technically, he is the best player I've ever seen."

Nothing Like the Cup

As any NHL player knows, breaking all the records in the world still doesn't touch the main goal: winning the Stanley Cup. The Oilers had been playing wonderfully and had finished first in their division. Playing in the first round against the Los Angeles Kings, the Oilers were expected to win without any problems. The Oilers somehow weren't up to the task. They blew early leads in two games, and let the Kings take the series, three games to two. It was a disappointing end to a great season, but it further solidified Wayne's goal to win a Cup.

Starting off the 1982–1983 season, fans were as full of criticism as they were of praise. Hockey, they said, should not be won with scores like 10–7 or 8–6. Some fans thought that scores like these were a direct result of Wayne's playing—a combination of heavy scoring and lapses in defense that would allow the opposing team to also run up high-scoring totals. Coach Sather played Wayne a few minutes less per game to ensure that his star player was fresh and energetic, and that his offensive and defensive games were more balanced.

His tactic worked. Edmonton again won its division and cruised through Winnipeg, Calgary, and Chicago in the playoffs, making the Stanley Cup finals after only four seasons in the NHL.

The Oilers' opponents in the finals were the New York Islanders, a team they had faced in the playoffs two years earlier, but never in such a high-profile, pressure-packed venue. This would be their biggest test to date. As it turned out, the Oilers were still too inexperienced and couldn't measure up to the Islanders' sheer determination.

The Islanders dove for the puck and basically "sacrificed" themselves for each win and, as a result of such grit, they swept the Oilers, four

This Wayne Gretzky doll, by Mattel, caters to Wayne's popularity among fans all across Canada.

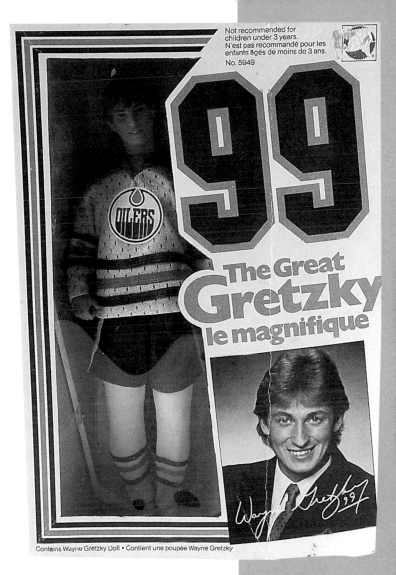

Not recommended for children under 3 years.
N'est pas recommandé pour les enfants âgés de moins de 3 ans.
No. 5949

99

The Great
Gretzky
le magnifique

Contains Wayne Gretzky Doll • Contient une poupée Wayne Gretzky

games to none. Wayne recalls seeing the Islanders' blackened eyes and bloody mouths in the locker room and saying, "They sacrificed everything they had."

Kevin Lowe, Wayne's roommate and teammate, agreed: "That's what wins championships." Wayne felt the loss deeply and apologized to his fans and teammates.

When he began the 1983–1984 season, Wayne had won nearly every award known to hockey, including four consecutive Hart

Trophies as league MVP. *Sports Illustrated* named him Sportsman of the Year, and Mattel had even made a Wayne Gretzky Doll in an effort to cash in on his huge appeal. But he still hadn't yet hoisted a Stanley Cup above his head. It became more than a goal for Wayne; it was his mission.

In the locker room, Oilers captain Lee Fogolin saw Wayne as an emerging leader. Tradition requires that the captain of each team wear a C on his jersey. In a move prophesized by Coach Sather years earlier, Fogolin removed the letter C from his shirt and handed it to Wayne. "I don't think there's anyone more deserving or prouder to take it than Wayne because he does so much for us on the ice," Fogolin announced. Wayne was honored and wore the C with pride. It looked as if the Oilers were now ready for the fight to the Cup.

The Great Point Streak

Despite an aching shoulder, Wayne scored early and often in the Oilers first games of the 1983–1984 season— so often, that for 51 games in a row, he continued racking up points in what became the longest game-point streak in NHL history. Wayne worked himself very hard during this streak. With a new record on the line in

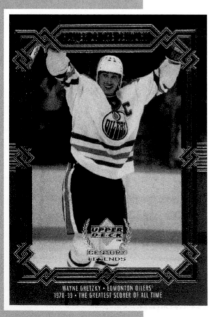

Following the Oilers' first appearance in the Stanley Cup finals, Lee Fogolin gave Wayne the letter C off of his own jersey in recognition of Wayne's leadership and talents on the ice. Wayne was now captain of the Edmonton Oilers.

BAD TIMING FOR THE GREAT ONE

Sports Illustrated magazine named Wayne "Sportsman of the Year" in 1982. Wayne thought this was a great honor, because people were recognizing not only his hockey skills but also his integrity and sportsmanship on the ice. Earlier that year, Wayne had been speaking out against fighting in hockey, a common practice that he resented. The night *Sports Illustrated* presented the award to Wayne, however, he got into a fight with Neal Broten of the Minnesota Wild. This was one of only a few fights that Wayne ever participated in during his career, and it certainly was made all the more embarrassing by its terrible timing! He remembers the fight as "the stupidest thing I ever did in my career."

every game, he didn't want to take the rest he greatly needed. People began to wonder if Wayne would score a point during every game of the 80-game season. Wayne's shoulder was worse every day and, at times, he couldn't move it at all.

When the streak ended with the 52nd game, Wayne was almost relieved, knowing he could finally rest his aching shoulder. The Oilers finished their season with Gretzky, Kurri, Coffey, and Messier each scoring over 100 points. Wayne led the team with 205 points. Even with these stellar performances backing them up, the Oilers were all business entering the playoffs. They swept Winnipeg and beat Calgary in seven games. After sweeping Minnesota four games to none in the semis, the Oilers were set for the finals against the Islanders.

A Moment to Savor

The Islanders were ready to play, but it was easy to notice something different about the Oilers this year. They were no longer an inexperienced bunch of kids. They were in their prime and led by the best hockey player in the world. In their first game, Edmonton won, 1–0. The Oilers lost 6–1 the following night, but came back with authority to win the next three games in front of Edmonton fans. Before game five, Wayne spoke to his team in the locker room. "I've had a lot of personal success. But nothing I've ever done means more than this." His words would later make history, as the Oilers ended the series with a 5–2 win over their longtime rivals. During the last few seconds of the game, Wayne remembers thinking, "This is going to be the most enjoyable moment of my life."

Fans went wild, not just in Edmonton, but all across Canada. The Oilers were finally Stanley Cup Champions. As Wayne hoisted the Cup above his head, he earned a place with his idol Gordie Howe and all other champions before him. This was how he wanted to be remembered. He skated a victory lap around the rink with the Cup and then, in true Gretzky style, he hoisted his younger brother Brent on his shoulders for a second trip. The following day, Gretzky, Messier, Lowe, and Coffey took the Cup into town, letting the people of Edmonton experience it in real life.

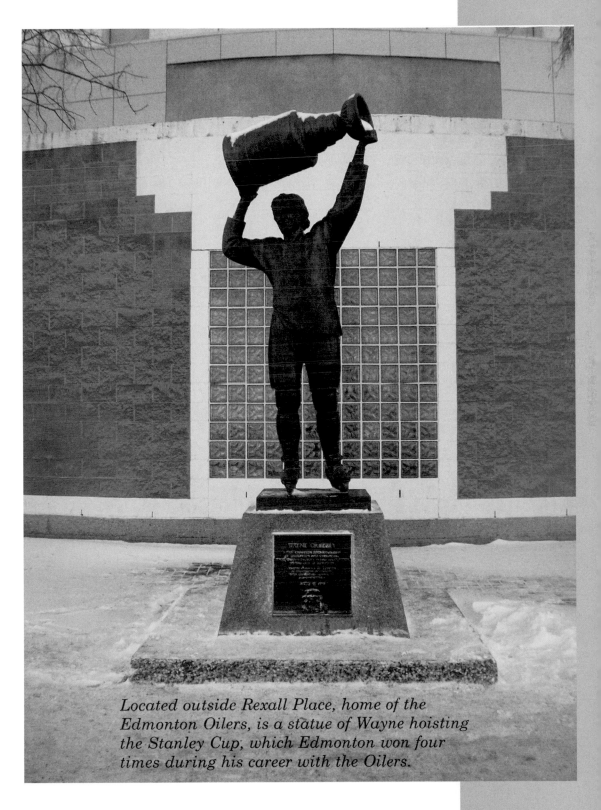

Located outside Rexall Place, home of the Edmonton Oilers, is a statue of Wayne hoisting the Stanley Cup, which Edmonton won four times during his career with the Oilers.

Chapter 4
The Trade Heard Around the World

After winning the Stanley Cup, Wayne and the Oilers were eager to defend their title. Fans expected the Oilers to start a dynasty with 23-year-old Wayne leading the way. But there were some unexpected detours on the Great One's road to continued success.

The Canada Cup

In the summer of 1984, Wayne had to pull out of his own celebrity charity tennis tournament to recover from surgery that removed bone chips from his ankle. He wanted to be in top shape for the Canada Cup, a tournament he remembers as his main focus at the time. He had always felt that playing for his country gave him a different feeling from any other experience on the ice, and he was eager to

After years of frustrating defeats by the Soviet Union, Team Canada, led by Wayne Gretzky, triumphed over their rivals in one of the most memorable tournaments in hockey history.

make his fellow Canadians proud. After years of frustrating defeats by the Soviet Union, Team Canada, led by Wayne Gretzky, triumphed over their rivals in one of the most memorable tournaments in hockey history. Wayne now had a Canada Cup to add to his name.

Moving into the season after the Canada Cup, Wayne seemed unstoppable, as did the Oilers. By December 1984, Wayne had scored six points in a single game against the Los Angeles Kings. This included his 1,000th point in the NHL. Before Wayne came along, Guy LaFleur had achieved this feat in 720 games. It took Wayne 424 games—a mere five seasons—to do the same. Wayne was redefining greatness. His biggest problem during this time wasn't scoring goals. It was the expectations of those around him. Wayne would often get "just" three goals in a single game and people began judging him, not by his performance in a league with hundreds of other players, but by what he had already accomplished.

Doing What It Takes

As Wayne's total points rose, so did his fame. He was interviewed for many magazines whose fans wanted the tiniest details of his routine. They wanted to know what he drank, how he dressed for games, and what time he went to bed every night. He gave his fans what they wanted and revealed his habits. Wayne soon became notorious for being superstitious, putting on his hockey gear in the same order before every game. His ritual must have worked, because the Oilers finished first in

*Members of Team Canada—all of them pro hockey players—
celebrate their triumph in the 1984 Canada Cup tournament
following their victory over their traditional rivals from the Soviet
Union. Shown here, from left, are Glenn Anderson, Brent Sutter,
Wayne Gretzky, Reggie Lemelin, and Peter Stastny.*

their division with 401 goals scored. For the third time, Wayne reached over 200 points. In 27 wins, the Oilers scored seven goals or more. Edmonton was headed for the playoffs—and another fight to the Stanley Cup.

In the first round of the 1984 playoffs, Edmonton swept the LA Kings, three games to none. Although it was a sweep, two of the games went into overtime.

The Oilers were stronger for playing the Kings and, in the next round, they swept the Jets as well. In the semifinals, they made the finals by beating Chicago in six games. Now only the Philadelphia Flyers stood between the Oilers and the Cup. Philly had the league's best regular-season record and played a very physical game. Their main goal was to slow down number 99.

The Oilers depended on speed to win, and Wayne even thought that Philadelphia purposely made its home ice choppy to slow his team down. If this was part of their plan, then it worked, and they held off Gretzky to a 4–1 Flyers win. The next day, however, it was an Edmonton newspaper article that captured the unhappiness of the hometown fans by calling the underachieving Oilers a "fraud."

A Cup on Home Ice

The Oilers needed their momentum back, and they needed it fast. Motivated by the newspaper article, they struggled defensively and evened out the series at one game a piece. In game three, Wayne scored two goals in the game's first two minutes and then added another for good measure before the period was over. They won again in game four, gaining a 3–1 series lead. Game five was set to be played on the Oilers' home ice in Edmonton.

Wayne and his team desperately wanted to win the Cup in front of their fans. It was an incredible night of hockey for Edmonton, with Wayne, Paul Coffey, and Jari Kurri all setting playoff scoring records. The Oilers clinched the Stanley Cup a second time with an 8–3 victory (the third time they scored eight points in the final game of a post-season series that year), proving once again that Gretzky was no flash in the pan. At the end of the 1984–1985 season, Wayne had won both the league and Stanley Cup MVP trophies.

The following year, 1985–1986, was one of Wayne's best. He surpassed his own points

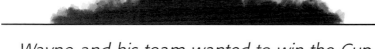

Wayne and his team wanted to win the Cup in front of their fans. It was an incredible night of hockey for Edmonton.

record with 215 and averaged more than two assists per game. He won his seventh-straight Hart Trophy as the league MVP. The Oilers dominated the first round of the playoffs, but soon trouble hit. During the second-round "Battle of Alberta" against the province's other big-city team, the Calgary Flames, the Oilers found themselves on the wrong side of the scoreboard. During the third period of game seven, Oiler defenseman Steve Smith accidentally banked the puck into the Oilers own net. This gave the Flames a 3–2 lead and the Oilers never recovered. It was a devastating loss for Wayne, and the early end to the season took a lot out of the team. The media were hard on Smith, but the Oilers refused to blame him.

After faltering in the 1986 playoffs, the Oilers were even more determined the next year. The 1987 Stanley Cup finals featured a dream matchup for fans, pitting the Oilers once again against the Flyers. Wayne and the Oilers had learned their lesson from the previous year. As Wayne put it, "The last thing we were going to do ... was be overconfident." The Oilers won the first two games on home ice. By the end of game six, however, the Oilers and Flyers were tied at three games apiece.

The buildup for game seven was enormous. The fans were buzzing, and both teams knew this was their last chance at victory. The Flyers had momentum coming out of a win in game six, but the Oilers had home ice. Within minutes of a Flyers goal, the Oilers tied the game. Soon after, Wayne and Kurri executed a perfect play, giving Edmonton a 2–1 lead. With the lead, the Oilers switched their focus to defense. They kept the Flyers at bay until the final three minutes and then scored a third goal, bringing the score to 3–1. As the buzzer sounded, the celebration began—the Oilers had won their third Cup!

After the victory, Wayne showed why he had won awards for sportmanship when he grabbed the Cup and immediately skated over to Steve

Smith. He knew Smith was still hurt from his 1986 playoff mistake and wanted him to be the first to raise the Cup. After the game, Wayne said, "It was the hardest Cup we have won."

The Best of the Best

Wayne's career hit another peak during the 1987 Canada Cup. Playing with and against the world's best hockey players, Wayne led Canada to the championship. He said this tournament might very well have been his best ever and, few could disagree, it established him as the best player in the world. In nine games he scored 21 goals—and yet, he wasn't the lead scorer of the tournament. That honor went to Mario Lemieux, who scored a total of 11 goals. Nine of these goals had been set up by his friend and teammate, number 99. Wayne was ecstatic for Mario, who was a rising star himself.

In 1988, the Oilers returned to claim the Stanley Cup again. The 1988 Cup was the Oilers' fourth in five years. The average Oiler age was 25. They were in their prime, and fans had now come to expect them to collect Cups for years to come. During the celebratory team photo on center ice, neither the players nor the fans had any idea that this would be the last time this remarkable group would be together as the Edmonton Oilers.

The Greatest Game

Even now, Wayne says that his greatest game might not have been a hockey game. He had no idea, while attending a basketball game in 1987 between the Los Angeles Lakers and

Boston Celtics, that this would also change his life. It was there that he met actor Janet Jones. The two had previously met before, but after being reintroduced at the basketball game, they quickly hit it off. They soon discovered that they had a lot in common. Janet's career as an actress and dancer had prevented her from having a normal childhood, much as Wayne's years on the ice had affected his youth. They had both experienced the trials and pressures of fame but, more importantly, they both longed for a normal life, complete with a family.

They went public with their relationship in 1987 as Janet accompanied Wayne to the Canada Cup. As Canadian fans watched, some

Many, including Oiler teammate Paul Coffey, felt that Wayne had been treated like a "piece of meat," and the city of Edmonton was shaken to the core.

were intrigued, while others were downright upset. Why did Wayne have to date an American woman? Soon after, the big news was announced. He had won his fourth Stanley Cup with the Oilers, but now Wayne was treading in new territory again. The Great One was getting hitched. When Wayne and Janet announced the news, the media quickly dubbed it "Canada's Royal Wedding."

HEIR TO GRETZKY'S THRONE: MARIO LEMIEUX

Born in Montreal in 1965, Mario Lemieux played for the Pittsburgh Penguins for 17 years. Despite his large size and strength, Mario was a quick skater and playmaker. His best season was during 1988–1989, where he was just one point shy of reaching Wayne's 200-point club. Mario was plagued by health problems, including tendinitis, chronic back pain and, most seriously, a type of cancer called Hodgkin's lymphoma. Although he was absent for many games because of his health, his skill remained high on the ice. After sitting out the entire 1994–1995 season, he returned the next season to win the Hart Trophy and the scoring title. Wayne also thought very highly of Lemieux, selecting him as the captain of Team Canada in the Olympic Winter Games in 2002. Following Lemieux's first retirement in 1997, the Hockey Hall of Fame waived the normal three-year waiting period and inducted him immediately into the Hall.

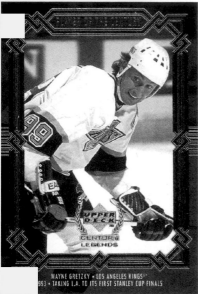

A trading card noting Wayne's career with the Los Angeles Kings

Over 700 people attended their July 1988 wedding in Edmonton. Another 200 people were there from the press, and thousands of fans gathered outside. Despite the huge expectations on them, the couple enjoyed themselves. Wayne remembers, "It was a tough wedding because we had to try to satisfy not only friends and family, we had to satisfy fans." With a new marriage, a great career, and a baby on the way, Wayne was on top of the world.

The Unthinkable

The happy celebration didn't last long. Despite Wayne's consistently spectacular performance, rumors had been surfacing about his future. Oilers owner Peter Pocklington was having financial troubles, and Wayne's salary was massive. In August 1988, less than a month after his wedding, it was announced in a heart-wrenching press conference that Wayne Gretzky had been traded to the Los Angeles Kings. The unofficial King of Hockey would now become a King in uniform as well, traded for two players, three first-round draft picks, and $15 million.

Many, including Oiler teammate Paul Coffey, felt that Wayne had been treated like a "piece of meat," and the city of Edmonton was shaken to the core. Even Wayne himself couldn't have been prepared for the reaction from Canadian fans. The city of Edmonton even erected a statue in his honor, placed outside the arena.

Controversy, charges, and accusations took over the media. Canadian fans and even other

Wayne Gretzky with wife, actor and dancer Janet Jones, at a 1989 NHL awards event. By this time, Wayne was playing for the Los Angeles Kings as a result of a trade that sent shock waves throughout the sports world, starting, of course, in Edmonton, Alberta,

"*You have to make people happy on both sides of the border. Sometimes it proved to be impossible, but I tried to wear both pairs of shoes.*"

Wayne Gretzky, on being a Canadian hockey star living and playing in the United States

players felt betrayed by Pocklington, who charged that it was Gretzky himself who wanted to be traded. Although Wayne would later admit that he chose the Kings, he was clear that he only made the choice after finding out he had no choice but to be traded. Despite wanting to finish his career with the Oilers, Wayne's decision was made for him.

The unthinkable had happened; the greatest player in the history of hockey had been traded. In one newspaper, the size of the headline was bigger than any other the paper had run since 1945 when World War II had ended. Feeling a sense of camaraderie and pride with their Canadian hero, many Canadian fans were heartbroken. Wayne Gretzky was Canada's national treasure, and now he would be playing for a U.S. team.

He knew it was coming—two hours after the Oilers' Stanley Cup victory, he was told that a trade was in the works—but Wayne didn't take the change much better: "I couldn't believe it was happening ... I won the [MVP], and all of a sudden, I'm traded."

Bringing Hockey to LA

Edmonton's loss was Los Angeles' gain, and soon Gretzky fever swept the United States. The moment he arrived in Los Angeles, he was a hot topic. The Kings made front-page news regularly, and talk of hockey became commonplace in newspapers and on television news shows. Many believed Wayne's effect would wear off, but ticket sales alone would prove them wrong. Season ticket sales soared, and Wayne's first game with the Kings drew 13,000 eager fans.

Some fans expected Wayne to single-handedly deliver Stanley Cup victories to the Kings, despite the fact that he had previously relied on his Oiler teammates for support.

Here he was in Edmonton, playing against the Oilers, and wearing a Kings jersey. It was like some kind of a dream.

He was, after all, the all-time leader in assists and this meant he needed teammates who could take advantage of his passes. His move to LA ice meant plenty of changes were in store for both Wayne and the Kings.

Wayne did help turn the Kings around. In his first game, he helped the Kings beat the Detroit Red Wings with one goal and three assists. This game got the Kings off to a four-game winning streak, and hockey was on its way to becoming popular in Los Angeles for the first time. People even dubbed it "Hockeywood." Although Wayne had been unable to turn Indianapolis into a hockey town in his younger years, he was certainly converting Los Angeles. He was also learning that being a Canadian hockey player living in the United States could be tough. He remembers, "You have to make people happy on both sides of the border. Sometimes it proved to be impossible, but I tried to wear both pairs of shoes."

A Moment of Truth

On October 19, 1988, Wayne suited up for a game he had been dreading for weeks. Here he was in Edmonton, playing against the Oilers, and wearing a Kings jersey. It was like some kind of a dream. He didn't know what to expect. How would his old fans and teammates respond to him? The moment he skated onto the ice, the reaction was clear. The Great One needn't have worried. He received a standing ovation. Wayne's relationship with his fans was solid, and that meant a lot to him.

Off the ice, Wayne had many Oiler friends, but on the ice it was a different story. They knew Wayne was their biggest threat, and they acted accordingly. Even his old friend Mark Messier slammed him into the boards twice. The Oilers won with a final score of 8–6. Wayne was glad the game was over.

By the end of the season, Wayne's effect on the Kings was evident. Their wins/losses/ties record of 42–31–7 would have been awful for the Oilers, but it gave the up-and-coming Kings reason to hope. Wayne had a total of 114 assists and 54 goals and another Hart Trophy as MVP. And, for the first time in his life, Wayne was off to the playoffs in a Kings jersey.

WAYNE GRETZKY • LOS ANGELES KINGS
1988-89 • A NEW KING MAKES A FAR-REACHING IMPACT

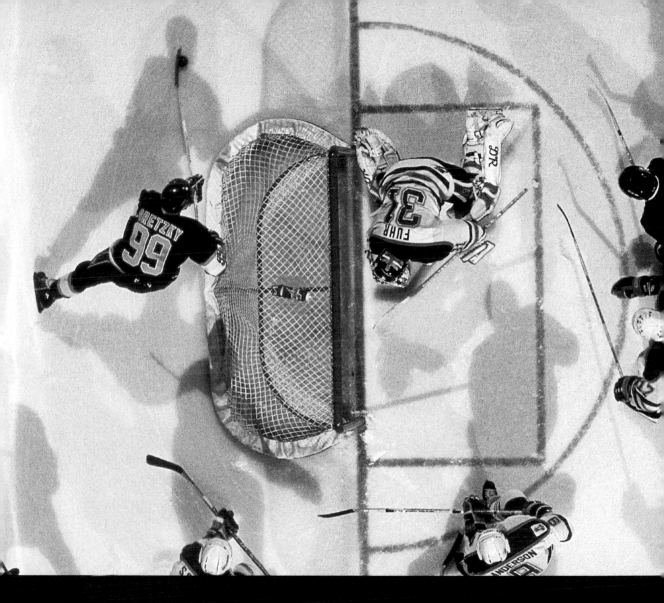

Wayne Gretzky, now wearing his famous number 99 for the LA Kings, sets up a shot from his "office" behind the net of his old team, the Edmonton Oilers. This photo was taken from above the ice in the first meeting of the two clubs in Edmonton since the trade that sent Wayne from Alberta to Southern California

SURPASSING MR. HOCKEY

When the Kings traveled to Edmonton on October 15, 1989, Wayne was one point shy of Gordie Howe's point record. He remembers, "It was the one record I wasn't sure I wanted to break. He's the best player ever and a part of me felt he should be remembered as having the most points ever." But he was so close, so early during the season it was only a matter of time.

Early in a game against the Oilers, Wayne got an assist to tie Howe. As the clock ticked down, Wayne skated in front of the Oilers net and backhanded the puck into the goal with less than a minute left. It was the very shot that Howe himself insisted Wayne practice, so many years earlier. The crowd erupted as even Oiler fans saddened by the loss of their hometown hero couldn't contain themselves. The game was stopped, and Howe came onto the ice with Wayne's family. His close friend Mark Messier gave him a diamond bracelet from the Oilers. The NHL and the Kings also gave him gifts. But with that 1,851st point, the Great One had earned more than gifts. He earned the respect of the league as a whole and that of his long-time idol. Gordie Howe had taken 1,767 games to reach his record. Wayne surpassed it in 780 games, and he had many more ahead of him.

Oh. The game? Well, Wayne's record-breaking goal tied the game at 4–4 with less than a minute to play in the third period. The winner? Los Angeles in overtime. The winning goal? In typical Wayne Gretzky fashion, scored by the Great One himself—as his 1,852nd career point.

> "It's a true honor to have my record broken by a man like Wayne Gretzky ... I couldn't be prouder."
>
> Gordie Howe

Wayne Gretzky of the Los Angeles Kings stands with Gordie Howe. They pose with the puck that Wayne used to pass Howe as the all-time point leader in the NHL against Wayne's old team, the Edmonton Oilers, on October 15, 1989, at Northlands Coliseum in Edmonton.

Chapter 5
The Great One's Final Games

When the 1990–1991 season rolled around, Wayne had been playing professional hockey for 12 years. Although 29 was young by normal standards, his extreme playing had resulted in his body beginning to show signs of wearing down.

Ready for the Cup?

Along with winning another Art Ross trophy for most total points in the season, Wayne also became the first NHL player to score 2,000 career points. The main barometer for Wayne's success was the impact he had on the Kings, and their improved play was a welcome sign that he was making a difference. For the first time since he switched jerseys, the Kings seemed prepared to fight for the Stanley Cup.

Wayne had led the Kings to the Stanley Cup finals for the first time in the club's history.

Los Angeles did indeed make the playoffs, and the Kings faced the Vancouver Canucks in the first round. After falling behind the Canucks two games to one, the Kings came back and won the next three games. Familiar faces met Wayne in the second round, where the Kings faced off against the defending champion Oilers, a team the Kings seemed destined to play often in various playoff series over the years.

The series began with fans on the edge of their seats. The Kings took game one, but it took an overtime period to do it. The next two games also went into overtime, with wins going to the Oilers. From there, the Oilers' momentum was too much, and the Kings eventually lost the series, four games to two. Wayne was reminded of how it felt to be on the losing team.

The following year seemed to repeat history. Wayne led the league in assists, but he scored only 31 goals. Los Angeles made the playoffs again, but was again sent home by the Oilers in six games. When the 1992–1993 season started, Wayne was plagued by another injury. After a professional-career total of 999 games, he learned from his doctors that he had a herniated disk and needed a year to recover completely.

Missing the season and another shot at the Cup were not in Wayne's plans. For 39 games, Wayne kept in shape and watched his team from the bench. He was pleased to see his team was doing well without him, with help from his old Oilers teammate Jari Kurri, whom the Kings had picked up in a trade. Wayne returned to the ice ahead of schedule and assisted with two goals in his first game. Throughout the second half of the season, there were no signs of his injury slowing him down. The Kings were again on their way to the playoffs.

First up was Calgary. The Kings scored 33 goals during their four-games-to-two series win. Vancouver, one of the best teams of the year, was up next. Riding on their momentum, the Kings won in six games. Advancing to the conference finals, the Kings geared up for the Maple Leafs. The Leafs gave the Kings a hard run, winning three of the first five games. In game six, Kings fans and players were on edge. The fans knew if they lost this game, the season was over. Finally, Wayne tied up the series and sent it to a seventh game with a power-play goal in overtime. Game seven would decide who went to the Stanley Cup finals.

A Trip to the Finals with the Kings

Game seven took place in Toronto, a place close to Wayne's heart. He was born just down the road from Maple Leaf Gardens and also remembered playing games there in his earlier years. He certainly didn't want the Kings season to end in front of his family and friends. He scored two goals early on and added an assist, giving the Kings a nerve-racking one-goal lead. In the third period, Wayne was in his "office" behind the net with the puck. He passed it, hoping it would reach a teammate's stick. Instead, it bounced off a Toronto player's skate and skipped into the net. Wayne didn't care how he scored, as long as the light lit up

behind the net signifying a goal! It was his third goal of the game, and the Kings went on to a 5–4 victory and a trip to the finals, where they would face the Montreal Canadiens.

Firing a wrist shot from the left side of the net, Wayne scored his 802nd career goal.

After winning four Stanley Cups with the Oilers and spending five seasons in Los Angeles scrabbling to make the playoffs, Wayne understood what a challenge it was first to get it into the playoffs, and then to advance. He was proud of his team for making it this far. He saw game seven of the Toronto series as "the best NHL game I ever played." Wayne had led the Kings to the Stanley Cup finals for the first time in the club's history. Montreal was a younger team and ended up taking the Kings in five games. Despite their incredible improvement, a Cup win was not in LA's future. For the first time, Wayne began to think about retiring.

The Last Record

The following season (1993–1994), Wayne was back on the ice. It was a difficult beginning, but he was nearing the last big record he had yet to break—Gordie Howe's career-goal mark of 801.

Wayne was getting close, but many off-ice distractions kept him from playing his best. His house was damaged by an earthquake in January, and his close friend and business partner, John Candy, died from a heart attack. At one point, he went seven games scoring only one point.

The record was finally his on March 23, 1994, in a game against Vancouver. Firing a wrist shot from the left side of the net, Wayne scored his 802nd career goal. As with his last big record-breaking play, officials stopped the game and his family joined him on the ice to celebrate. Fans cheered and celebrated along with him, as they had his entire career.

Locked Out

The Kings missed the playoffs that season, but Wayne had forgotten about wanting to retire. The time had come for another collective bargaining agreement (CBA) to be worked out between players and owners. The CBA covers all aspects of NHL player employment, dealing with salary caps, or limits, and much more. When both sides were unable to come to an agreement, the owners began canceling games in the 1994–1995 season.

With the season schedule now reduced to 48 games, Wayne found himself with some extra time on his hands. Taking matters into his own hands, he did something that no other player had ever attempted. He organized a team of his own called the Ninety-Nine All-Stars. The team, including his friend Mark Messier, played teams from other countries. He saw the tour as a good way to stay in shape and keep morale up, but it accomplished much more than this.

Throughout Europe, Wayne and the All-Stars got a great reception, with European fans greeting them with open arms. He had no idea how popular he and the NHL would be in Europe. The All-Stars won most of their games but, more importantly, they ran daily clinics, signed autographs, and showcased their players. Typically, in pro sports, the mood after a lockout is somber and hostile, but in the weeks following the tour of Wayne and his All-Stars, the mood in hockey was optimistic, if not cheerful. He had reminded people what hockey could be about, focusing on the love of the game instead of money.

After the lockout, the Kings played terribly, winning only 11 games in the shortened season. They missed the playoffs for the second year in a row. Wayne was starting his eighth season with the Kings and soon he would be a free agent. Realizing that he was nearing the end of his contract with Los Angeles, and possibly the end of his career, Wayne desperately wanted to play for a team that would contend for the Stanley Cup. If he stayed and played out his contract with the Kings, he felt certain he wouldn't have another trip to the finals. Rumors began to surface of a trade.

Briefly Blue in St. Louis

During the trading period in the off-season, the Kings knew that they had virtually no chance of signing Wayne again and didn't want to lose such a valuable property to free agency without getting anyone in return. So they gave

Wayne gives a thumbs-up as he holds up the puck he used to score his 802nd NHL goal—and break another record previously held by Gordie Howe—on March 23, 1994.

in and traded Wayne to the St. Louis Blues. It was a surprise move. Most of the hockey world had expected him to join his old teammate Mark Messier on the New York Rangers. During his first moments with St. Louis, Wayne said:

"I'm emotionally drained. I'm disappointed to be leaving Los Angeles, but I'm excited to play in St. Louis."

The Blues were happy to have Wayne on their team, and captain Shayne Corson immediately gave him the "C" off his jersey. Wayne was set to be team captain of his third NHL team.

The first week of the 1995–1996 started off with a bang for Wayne—or, more specifically, a knock-out. During his second game, he was hit in the head by an elbow from the Oilers' Kelly Buchberger. The hit knocked him out cold and resulted in a small concussion. Later in the season, he was checked by Doug Gilmour, received a contusion, and missed three games. The Blues made the playoffs and, in the first round against the Maple Leafs, Wayne was hit constantly. Clearly, the Leafs knew where the heart of their competition lay.

Despite the punishment, Wayne and the Blues made it past Toronto, taking four out of six games, and faced off against the powerful Detroit Redwings in the second round. The teams battled to game seven, with the Blues dropping a heartbreaker in double overtime with a score of 1–0. A few fans and members of the media blamed Wayne publicly for some of the losses, and he didn't disagree:

*"I stink. It's my responsibility to
lead this team, and I consider
myself responsible for both those losses."*

After the loss, Wayne decided to leave
the Blues. He was a free agent and
could sign with any team he chose.
Many wanted him to join the Oilers
again, so he could finish his career
where it had started. On July 22, 1996,
however, Wayne announced he had
signed on with the New York Rangers
for two years.

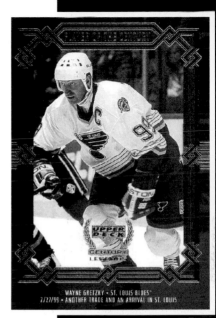

WAYNE GRETZKY · ST. LOUIS BLUES
2/27/99 · ANOTHER TRADE AND AN ARRIVAL IN ST. LOUIS

A New York State of Mind

Wayne's move to Manhattan was fitting.
He had gone from Canada to the glitz and
glamour of Los Angeles, and now he was
moving to the sophisticated east coast. He
admitted that, along with the chance to play
in a championship again, the shot to play with
his old teammate Mark Messier was what had
tipped the scales.

Before the season started, Wayne got to join
Messier in representing his country once again.
The World Cup had replaced the Canada Cup,

*This trading
card notes
Wayne's stint as
a member of the
St. Louis Blues
in 1996.*

*Many critics believed that the Rangers—and
Wayne—were just getting too old.*

and Team Canada was a favorite to win. Again, Wayne was the team captain and, his old Oilers coach, Glen Sather, had even come to watch. When he watched Gretzky and Messier reunite, he said "They were like a couple of brothers who hadn't seen each other in a long, long time." Although Team Canada didn't win the World Cup, Wayne felt a fresh energy while playing with his old friend.

In 1998, Wayne was selected to play for Team Canada in the Winter Olympics in Japan ... he was eager not to disappoint his Canadian fans.

During Wayne's first season with the Rangers, from 1996–1997, he and Messier led the team to the playoffs. During that season Wayne also tied for the league lead in assists. The year 1997 brought another change to the Rangers when Messier, now a free agent, signed with Vancouver during the summer.

One of the main reasons Wayne had joined the Rangers was to play hockey alongside Messier. He was no longer scoring 200 points a season, and partnering with Messier took some of the attention off of him. When Messier left, Wayne found himself in the spotlight again. He wasn't team captain, but fans now saw Wayne alone as the driving force behind the success or failure of the Rangers. The following two

Wayne Gretzky's last stop on his journey in professional hockey was a three-season stint with the New York Rangers.

seasons were unremarkable, and many critics believed that the Rangers—and Wayne—were just getting too old.

Part of the problem with Wayne's performance was the lack of a support system on the ice. While he could no longer rely on his speed to get points, his passing was still flawless. His perfect passes often fell onto open ice, however. When Messier left, he took with him a special, instinctive connection with Wayne. With no one to take advantage of Wayne's ability to create points with his assists, the media speculated that he might indeed be headed for retirement.

Olympic Hopefuls

In 1998, Wayne was selected to play for Team Canada in the Winter Olympics in Japan. It was the first year NHL players were allowed to compete. This was a new opportunity for Wayne, and he was eager not to disappoint his Canadian fans.

When the Canadian team arrived in Japan, Wayne was swamped with attention. The fans and media came from far and wide to see the Great One in action, hopeful that he would represent his country well. Despite a good start, Team Canada didn't make it to the gold-medal game. During a shoot-out in the semifinals, Wayne wasn't chosen to shoot against Czech goalie Dominik Hasek. Canada lost 2–1 and later competed against Finland for the bronze medal. Losing to Finland, Team Canada came out of the Olympics empty-handed. Coming from the Land of Hockey, Wayne, Team Canada, and fans alike were bitterly disappointed. After losing a chance at

A Teammate for Life: Mark Messier

Wayne called Mark "Moose" Messier the best player he ever played with. Together on the Oilers, Messier and Gretzky were a powerful team, working together to score goals and protect each other on the ice. Mark stepped up as the Oilers' star when Wayne left, earning the second spot on the all-time career list for points scored during the regular season. He also won six Stanley Cups, five with the Oilers and one with the New York Rangers. Even while playing on opposing teams, Wayne and Mark held each other in the highest regard. In 1996, Wayne joined Mark on the New York Rangers, eager to play again with his right-hand man.

the gold medal, Wayne said, "This is a crushed locker room right now and probably a crushed country." He felt the disappointment of a nation on his shoulders.

The End of an Era

By the spring of 1999, Wayne knew in his heart he was nearing the end of his professional career. He didn't want to fade away like many other professional athletes, growing tired and worn before the fans. Wayne also wanted to thrive in his retirement, without any serious physical injuries. Rumors started circulating that Wayne would soon call it quits, and that April 18 would be his last day on the ice.

Fans were devastated. On April 15, playing

against the Ottawa Senators in what was thought to be his last game on Canadian ice, fans crowded the stands with homemade signs that read, "Say It Ain't So, Wayne" and "Gretzky Is God." There had been no official announcement yet, but Gretzky fever took full rein of the crowd. After the game ended in a

He had taken off his NHL skates thousands of times in the past 21 years, but this time was different.

tie, fans went wild. Wayne was brought to center ice with tears in his eyes for three encores. He remembers, "That's when it hit me that I'm retired."

The following day, the official announcement was made. At a tearful press conference reminiscent of his Kings trade announcement, Wayne announced that April 18 would be his last game-playing day: "My gut, my heart is telling me this is the right time." Just as he had hundreds of times as a kid, he rode with his dad to his last hockey game.

Many special guests arrived to watch history in the making, including his family, Coach Sather, Mark Messier, and Mario Lemieux. Both the Canadian and U.S. national anthems were sung, changing the lyrics to include

Wayne Gretzky skates for Team Canada against Sergei Stas of Belarus during the Winter Olympic Games in Nagano, Japan, on February 13, 1998. Although Canada beat Belarus 5–0, the Canadians failed to win any medals, bitterly disappointing fans, members of the team, and people across Canada.

Wayne's name in both. Although Wayne was ready to play his last game, it seemed that the world couldn't fathom hockey without the Great One.

In that game, the Rangers lost to the Penguins in overtime, but the score was the last thing on anyone's mind. As he took his celebration laps around the rink, Wayne took in the moment and said these words:

"I've been so fortunate to play with some of the greatest players ... like the best player I ever played against, Mario Lemieux ... my teammates and, of course, the best player I ever played with, Mark Messier."

Although he was confident in his decision to retire, Wayne had mixed emotions in the locker room after the game. He had taken off his NHL skates thousands of times in the past 21 years, but this time was different. After hanging up his skates for the last time, Wayne stayed in his equipment for another hour and a half. He knew the world of hockey would never be the same, but he also recognized that his own life was about to change.

Opposite: The front page of the New York Daily News *on Monday, April 19, 1999, says it all.*

DAILY ◉ NEWS

50¢   www.nydailynews.com   NEW YORK'S HOMETOWN NEWSPAPER   Monday, April 19, 1999

FAREWELL!

Tears flow at the Garden as Great One plays his final game

Wayne Gretzky
salutes more than
18,000 who came
to say goodbye
yesterday

COREY SIPKIN DAILY NEWS

COVERAGE ON PAGES 2-3 AND SPORTS

Chapter 6
A Legacy On and Off the Ice

It didn't take long for the Great One to be immortalized in legend. Seven days after retiring his skates, Wayne was informed he was to be inducted in the Hockey Hall of Fame in Toronto. Normally, there is a three-year waiting period before a retired player can be inducted, but the Hall of Fame waived the rule for the Great Gretzky.

The Changes Begin

Twenty-five hundred people packed into the Hall to see his induction. Years earlier, 12-year-old Wayne used to sneak into the Hall to admire and stare at memorabilia from the hockey greats. On November 22, 1999, Wayne got to see his own equipment up there with the

On November 22, 1999, Wayne got to see his own equipment up there with the others', lining the walls of the Hall.

others', lining the walls of the Hall. He was officially alongside his greatest idols.

Wayne's life continued to change after his retirement, although he was still very much involved with the game of hockey. He and Janet had already had three children, Paulina, Ty, and Trevor. In 2000, Janet gave birth to another son, Tristan. Three years later, Emma Marie was born. The Gretzky family was growing and happy. Although many fans wondered if any of his children would take up hockey, Wayne was careful not to push is children into any sport.

Behind the Glass

Although he was off the ice, Wayne was still in love with the game. In the summer of 2000, he collaborated with Steve Ellman, who was buying the NHL's Phoenix Coyotes. Wayne took a part-owner's share of the team and was put in charge of the team's hockey operations. Just like the Oilers, the Coyotes had their roots in the WHA. They started out as the Winnipeg Jets and moved to Phoenix in 1996. When Wayne became part owner, the Coyotes had struggled for years, remaining the oldest NHL team to never appear in a Stanley Cup final.

Representing Canada Again

Wayne also took on another challenge during 2000, taking over the management of Team Canada as Executive Director. The 2002 Winter Olympics were set for Salt Lake City, and Wayne was in charge of hand-picking players and coaches to represent the nation.

He remembered his own Olympic journey

WAYNE GRETZKY
1978-99 • THE ULTIMATE ALL-STAR

Wayne Gretzky as an All-Star

Wayne Gretzky (in the dark suit at the center of this photo) as coach of the Phoenix Coyotes in a game against the Detroit Red Wings. Wayne had bought a share of ownership in the Coyotes in 2000, and following a labor dispute that shut down the entire NHL season in 2004–2005, he took over the head coaching duties on his team during the next season.

well, and he knew there would be just as much media frenzy in 2002. Team Canada had a hard time in previous competitions and, in 2002, it started out with a mediocre 1–1–1 record. When the media attacked his team, Wayne fought back. He told them not to judge Team Canada so quickly. He was right, and the media would soon be eating their words.

After making it to the gold-medal game against the United States, the pressure was on. A rivalry had developed between Canada

and the United States, and Team Canada
fought hard. In that final game, Wayne
watched from the stands as Team Canada beat
the United States, 5–2. It was Canada's first
Olympic gold medal in 50 years. Once again,
the Great Gretzky was a Canadian hero. He
would later recall that, second only to his first
Stanley Cup, winning that Olympic medal was
one of his greatest hockey moments.

Stepping Up

It seemed as though all of Wayne's experience
on the ice had made him an effective coach.
After a difficult labor disagreement, the entire
2004–2005 NHL season was canceled. Coming
into the next season, the league badly needed
to lighten the spirits of the fans. Just as he did
after the labor dispute of 1999, Wayne stepped
up and made a change. He announced that he
would take over as head coach of the Coyotes.
Even marginal fans seemed more drawn to
hockey whenever Wayne was involved, so
just having him on board was a big boost
to the league.

Many experts thought the Coyotes would
remain the NHL's worst team, but they
finished surprisingly well. They stayed
in contention for the playoffs for most of
the season before falling short toward the
end. In the middle of this modest success,
however, Wayne's life would soon take a
devastating turn.

In December 2005, at the age of 64, Wayne's
mother, Phyllis, lost her battle with lung
cancer. She had been diagnosed in the autumn
of 2004, and the entire Gretzky family had

Members of Team Canada, including head coach Pat Quinn (top, center, in the dark suit) and NHL legend Wayne Gretzky (top, upper left, also in a dark suit), celebrate their 5–2 victory over the United States in the gold-medal round of the 2002 Winter Olympics in Salt Lake City, Utah. In 2000 Wayne took on the job of hand-picking the players and coaching staff of Team Canada.

Wayne remembers, "Throughout my career, she was in the background, but she was the glue."

rallied at her side. Wayne announced an indefinite leave from coaching, and his siblings joined him in the hospital. Wayne remembers, "Throughout my career, she was in the background, but she was the glue." Canadians everywhere mourned the loss along with Wayne and his family.

Shortly after his mother's death, many wondered if Wayne would return to coaching. The Winter Olympics were approaching again, and he signed on to coach Team Canada. It was during this time in 2006 that he was hit with another shock. His wife, Janet, was caught in a very public gambling scandal for allegedly placing bets on sporting events.

A Rough Time

Both Janet and Wayne were caught up in a media frenzy. As Janet was the wife of an NHL coach, it became about much more than placing a few small bets of one's own. Many also thought Janet was making bets on Wayne's behalf, although she repeatedly denied this. Wayne stood by his wife through this time, and eventually investigators agreed that he had no involvement with the gambling. Much damage had already been done, and some people now questioned his integrity. He had maintained a pristine reputation during his entire career, so having to defend himself to the public was new and uncomfortable for him.

Wayne was once again Executive Director with the Canadian men's hockey team, and he was hopeful that the upcoming Winter Olympics would provide a new start in his relationship with the media and the public. Team Canada lost to Russia in the quarterfinals, however, and didn't get to play for a medal.

When things went well for Team Canada, fans were eager to praise Wayne. When things went badly in 2006, they were just as eager to criticize him. He took full responsibility for the loss and reminded people that Team Canada would be back in 2010. He also signed on for another five-year deal as Phoenix's head coach.

Although he did not return to work in an official capacity with Team Canada in 2010, Wayne was given another great honor. He was asked to represent his country on the worldwide stage, officially lighting the Olympic Torch during the Opening Ceremonies in Vancouver. He also watched with pride alongside thousands of fans as Team Canada won the gold medal game against the United States, with a final score of 3–2. He had been right—they were back.

The Great Gretzky

On ice, Wayne redefined what people thought was possible. He broke every record known to hockey. He used the ice in new and innovative ways, being the first player to use the space behind the net. He had a sense of anticipation that often seemed extrasensory. Many experts have described his physical skill as poetry on ice. Captaining three NHL teams, he not only expected the best from himself but also brought it out in his teammates and opponents. As far as skill is concerned, nobody has or likely will come close to his achievements in hockey.

Wayne also changed the face of professional hockey around the world. Before he joined the Los Angeles Kings, hockey was often seen as "Canada's game." Although Canadians are still patriotic about their love of hockey, Gretzky opened up the sport for the rest of North America. Even in Europe, the Great Gretzky reigns as hockey's king.

Over the years, perfect passes and ESP-like anticipation turned out to be just the beginning. Although he demolished the record books, maintaining his integrity throughout his career might have been his truest, highest achievement. In an age where professional athletes are often led by their egos, Wayne represented his sport and his country with integrity, class, and dignity. Goals, assists, and points break the records, but attitude becomes a legacy. Wayne learned early on that the way he behaved off the ice was just as important as how he behaved on it. He learned this from his idol Gordie Howe and, of course, his own father. Wayne was always grounded and friendly, and he showed sportsmanship at almost every turn.

It Runs in the Family

Wayne credits much of his success to his loving and supportive family. In particular, his father played a key role in his personal and professional life. Whenever Wayne needed support, he was there with wise words and unconditional love. He also knew when Wayne needed tough love. When Wayne's lackluster performance helped cost the Oilers the Stanley Cup in 1983, Walter pointed to Wayne's grandmother at work puttering in the garden. With that one motion, Walter impressed on Wayne the importance of consistent diligence in working toward a goal, whatever that goal may be.

Walter has been involved in charitable causes, and his honesty, decency, and integrity have made him one of the most recognized and respected men in Canada. In 2008, Walter received the Order of Canada, an award that recognizes the distinguished service of Canadians on behalf of their country and humankind in general.

"Goals, assists, and points break the records, but attitude becomes a legacy."

Wayne supports a variety of children's charities aimed at helping disadvantaged kids play sports because he knows firsthand the positive effect sports can have on youth. His own charity, the Wayne Gretzky Foundation, has raised over one million dollars to support youth in hockey.

"I owe everything I have to hockey. It's given me ... a chance to see the world, to meet some great people. I get paid a lot of money for something that I love to do. And when you think you're bigger than the sport, you're in trouble."

Wayne Gretzky

Hockey may never see another Wayne Gretzky. Some of his records may be broken, and other players will join him in the Hockey Hall of Fame. But his contagious spirit, calm confidence, and tucked-in jersey will always be remembered as the trademarks of a man who could bring together a nation whenever he took to the ice to play the sport he loved and respected. The Great Gretzky will remain etched in history as the greatest hockey player the world has ever seen.

Canadian hockey legend Wayne Gretzky lights the Vancouver 2010 Olympic torch on February 12, 2010, at the end of the opening ceremony.

Chronology

1961 Wayne Douglas Gretzky is born in Brantford, Ontario, on January 26.

1967 Wayne begins playing novice hockey and scores his first-ever goal.

1972 Wayne earns the name "The Great Gretzky," scoring 378 goals in 85 games. He meets his idol, Gordie Howe, for the first time.

1975 Wayne moves from Brantford, Ontario to Toronto, Ontario.

1977 Wayne officially wears jersey number 99. He will keep this number for the rest of his hockey career.

1978 Wayne wins Rookie of the Year honors for the Ontario Hockey Association. He signs with the Indianapolis Racers of the World Hockey Association (WHA).

1979 Wayne is traded to the Edmonton Oilers, also of the WHA. Following the 1978–1979 season, the WHA folds, and four WHA teams, Edmonton among them, become part of the National Hockey League (NHL).

1980 Wayne wins his first Hart Memorial Trophy as Most Valuable Player in the NHL. It will be his first of nine.

1981–1982 Wayne sets a new record, scoring 50 goals in 39 games.

1983–1984 The "Great Point Streak" begins as Wayne scores the first goal on his way to scoring points in 51 straight games.

1984 Wayne leads the Edmonton Oilers to their first Stanley Cup victory in franchise history.

1985 The Edmonton Oilers win their second Stanley Cup.

1987 Wayne scores his 1,500th career point. He is the fourth in NHL history to reach this number. Wayne and the Oilers win their third Stanley Cup.

1988 Wayne marries actress Janet Jones in Canada's "Royal Wedding." Wayne wins what will be his last Stanley Cup. Following the 1987–1988 season, he is traded to the Los Angeles Kings. Paulina, his daughter, is born.

1989 Wayne breaks Gordie Howe's record, becoming the NHL's all-time points leader.

1990 Ty Gretzky is born.

1992 Suffering from a herniated disc in his back, Wayne is off the ice for eight months. Trevor Gretzky is born.

1993 Wayne leads the Los Angeles Kings to the Stanley Cup finals.

1994 Wayne becomes the NHL's all-time leader in goals scored. After an NHL lockout, he leads the "Ninety-Nine All-Star" tour.

1996 Knowing that Wayne has only one year left before becoming a free agent, the Kings trade him to the St. Louis Blues. After one season, he signs with the New York Rangers as a free agent.

1998 Wayne plays for Team Canada in the Winter Olympics in Nagano, Japan.

1999 Wayne plays his last NHL game, and the number 99 is retired. Wayne is officially inducted into the Hockey Hall of Fame.

2000 Tristan Gretzky, Wayne's son, is born.

2001 Wayne becomes managing partner of the Phoenix Coyotes.

2002 Team Canada, coached by Wayne, wins gold at the Winter Olympics.

2003 Emma Gretzky, Wayne's youngest daughter, is born.

2005 Taking on a new hockey challenge, Wayne becomes coach of the Phoenix Coyotes. Wayne's mother succumbs to lung cancer at the age of 64.

2006 Wayne's wife, Janet, is involved in a sports betting scandal. Neither she nor Wayne are charged with any wrongdoing. Wayne again coaches Team Canada in the Winter Olympics. Canada is eliminated in the quarterfinals and fails to win a medal.

2007 Wayne and Janet launch a winery, No. 99 Estates Winery.

2008 Wayne's father, Walter, receives the Order of Canada. Wayne opens a restaurant in Toronto called Gretzky's.

2010 Wayne is chosen to light the Olympic torch at the Opening Ceremonies of the Winter Olympics in Vancouver, British Columbia.

Glossary

barometer Something that records or indicates changes

Canada Cup In hockey, an invitational international tournament that was held on five occasions. The last Canada Cup tournament took place in 1991.

concussion An injury to the brain from a fall or hit, usually resulting in loss of consciousness

draft In hockey, selecting new players from a group of amateur players by teams at a higher level

dynasty In sports, a powerful team with continued success over a period of time

grueling Difficult, bringing one to exhaustion

Junior A In Canadian hockey, the levels of competition for amateur players between the ages of 16 and 20, including members of the Ontario Hockey League

Junior B In Canadian hockey, the levels of competition for amateur players below the skill level of the Junior A teams.

Instead of a single trophy, these teams compete for various trophies across the country.

lockout In sports, a work stoppage that occurs when team owners prevent their players from playing games, usually during a labor dispute

momentum A tendency to go forward repeating recent success. The Oilers had momentum after winning the Stanley Cup.

National Hockey League (NHL) A professional hockey league consisting of a number of U.S. and Canadian teams. The Stanley Cup is awarded to the league champion at season's end.

novice In hockey, a league for beginners usually under nine years of age

Ontario Hockey Association A group once composed of four tiers of hockey. As of 1980, the Junior A teams became known as the Ontario Hockey League, leaving the three remaining tiers.

Ontario Minor Hockey Association The largest minor-level hockey association in the world. The OMHA is the governing body for several Ontario leagues.

Peewee A minor level of hockey competition for players below the Junior age level, typically 11–12

pickup games Games that are not part of a regularly scheduled competition. Wayne often played pickup games with his friends in his backyard rink, called Wally Coliseum.

pristine Remaining unspoiled, pure, or clean

prodigy A person, often a child, having extraordinary talent in a field, such as sports, music, or dance

rookie An athlete playing his or her first season in a league or on a team

scout A person who watches and reports on specific players. Scouts often recommend new talent for recruitment.

showboating Showing off, looking for attention

Stanley Cup The highest honor in the National Hockey League, a trophy awarded to the playoff champion. It is also referred to as "The Cup" or "Lord Stanley's Cup."

stick handling Moving the puck along the ice with a hockey stick

sweep To win every game in a series

tonsillitis Inflammation of the tonsils, often resulting in their removal by minor surgery

uncanny Characterized by a mysterious or inexplicable power or ability

unfathomable Difficult or impossible to understand

veteran In sports, characterized by having played for years and having gained considerable experience

World Hockey Association (WHA) A professional hockey league that existed from 1972 to 1979 consisting of a number of U.S. and Canadian teams. Four WHA teams joined the NHL in 1979.

Further Information

Books

Benson, Michael. *Wayne Gretzky: Hockey Player.*
New York, NY: Ferguson, 2004.

Brunt, Stephen. *Gretzky's Tears: Hockey, America and the Day Everything Changed.*
Chicago, IL: Triumph Books, 2009.

Doeden, Matt. *Wayne Gretzky.* (Sports Legends).
Minneapolis, MN; Twenty-first Century Books, 2007.

Gretzky, Wayne, and Rick Neilly. *Gretzky: An Autobiography of Wayne Gretzky.*
Toronto: HarperCollins, 1990.

Morrison, Scott. *Wayne Gretzky: The Great Goodbye.*
Toronto: Key Porter Books, 1999.

Web sites

http://espn.go.com/blog/sportscenter/tag/_/name/wayne-gretzky
The history and career of Wayne Gretzky is documented on this site, which includes links to hockey highlights, interviews, and "This Day in History" features.

www.gretzky.com/
Wayne Gretzky is still very much active in the hockey community, with an updated site featuring the latest news and information about his career. It provides links to photos, player profiles, and a detailed interactive timeline.

http://nhl.com/ice/player.htm?id=8447400
This site is maintained by the National Hockey League. It provides player links as well as detailed career profiles, video, news headlines, and other hockey information.

www.hhof.com/
The Hockey Hall of Fame is a 57,000-square-foot (5,295 sq m) museum and hall of fame that exhibits hockey memorabilia. Located in Toronto, Ontario, the HHOF maintains an updated website outlining its current and future exhibits. Many hockey stars of the past are featured, including Wayne Gretzky, Mario Lemieux, Mark Messier, and Gordie Howe.

DVDs

Lord Stanley's Cup (DVD). Warner Home Video, 2003.

NHL Greatest Moments (DVD). Warner Home Video, 2006.

NHL: Just Like Me—Profile of NHL Legends and the New Crop of NHL Stars (2008) (DVD). Warner Home Video, 2008.

NHL Overtime: Heroes and Drama of the Stanley Cup Playoffs (Vintage Hockey Collection) (DVD). Warner Home Video, 2006.

NHL's Greatest Goals (Vintage Hockey Collection) (DVD). Warner Home Video, 2006.

Ultimate Gretzky 4-disc Special Edition (2003) (DVD). Warner Home Video, 2006.

Index

Index

About the Author

Jessica Morrison is a Canadian writer, educator, and sculptor living in Toronto, Ontario. She attended the University of Guelph for a degree in Zoology and a Masters of Science degree. The author of numerous nonfiction books for children, she is constantly on the lookout for people and places with a story to tell. She has also written on Hank Aaron for Crabtree Publishing and is currently writing her first novel.